FEARSOME
FOREST
FIRES

Jane Katirgis and Michele Ingber Drohan

Enslow Publishing
101 W. 23rd Street
Suite 240
New York, NY 10011
USA

enslow.com

WORDS TO KNOW

ecosystem—The special way that plants and animals function together in nature.

ember—A piece of wood that glows in the ashes of a fire.

myth—A story that tells how things in nature were made.

oxygen—A colorless gas that makes up part of the air we breathe.

parachute—To jump out of an airplane with an umbrella-like object on your back.

Pulaski—A tool that looks like an ax and a hoe that is used by firefighters to make a fire line.

remote—Far away.

sacred—Highly respected and very important.

shingle—A thin piece of material that covers the roof of a house.

threaten—To be a possible cause of harm.

CONTENTS

This Buddhist temple shows how fire is still sacred today.

1

FLAMES
OF FIRE

All through history, fire has been important to people. Many believe fire is **sacred**. This is because it gives warmth, but it can also cause harm. Different cultures all over the world have **myths** about fire. Myths are stories. Some myths tell how things in nature came to be.

The most famous myth about fire comes from ancient Greece. This myth tells how fire was stolen from the gods who ruled over earth and was then given to humans. Today we know that fire is something that happens in nature and it was on the earth long before people were.

WHAT IS FIRE?

Fire is the flame, heat, and light that we see when something is burning. Fire needs three things to burn. These things are a gas called **oxygen**, fuel,

COLORADO FOREST FIRES OF 2012

It turned out that 2012 was a record-setting year in Colorado. There was more damage from forest fires than in any other year. The fire departments counted 4,167 forest fires. One of them was the biggest the state had ever seen.

A very long heat wave and lots of wind made fighting these fires very hard. Tens of thousands of people had to leave their homes. It was not safe for them to stay during the fires.

Forest fires burn in Colorado during the worst year of fires the state had ever seen.

Fire brings warmth to people's homes.

and heat. Oxygen comes from the air we breathe. Fuel comes from things that burn, such as wood, leaves, and paper. When oxygen and fuel mix with heat, a fire starts.

Fire is very useful. We cook food with it, and it heats our homes. But fire is also very powerful. It can be dangerous when it gets out of control.

2

A FOREST FIRE BEGINS

There are different ways that forest fires can start. Sometimes they are started by natural causes. This can happen when lightning hits a tree in a forest and starts a fire. This occurs a lot because there are more than 40,000 lightning storms each year all over the world.

PEOPLE ARE USUALLY TO BLAME

Most forest fires are started by people. In fact, four out of every five forest fires are caused by people. If someone doesn't put out a cigarette or

If you build a campfire, be sure to put it out completely. Otherwise, it could start a forest fire.

if a campfire is left burning by a camper, a forest fire can start easily. If people were more careful, we could prevent most forest fires.

LIGHTNING STRIKES IN CALIFORNIA

It was the summer of 2008. There were more than 3,500 wildfires burning in California. Most of the fires started with lightning strikes. Also, it had been very dry in California. This made it easier for the land to catch on fire. The extra wind in this season helped spread the fires too.

Lots of forests and other land burned. Thirty-two people were killed. Many countries around the world wanted to help, including Australia, Canada, and Mexico. They sent money to help the United States fight the fires.

One natural cause of forest fires is lightning.

3

WHAT TYPE OF FOREST FIRE IS IT?

Not all forest fires are the same. There are three different types. A ground fire burns slowly. It moves along the ground using leaves and moss as fuel. You don't see many flames in a ground fire. You might only see glowing **embers** on the forest floor. A surface fire burns more quickly. It also stays close to the ground. But it uses branches as fuel, and it can burn and kill trees. A crown fire is the worst kind of fire. It climbs up trees and

A surface fire moves through the forest floor.

moves very fast. Crown fires move from treetop to treetop as fast as ten miles an hour.

BRUSH FIRES

Brush fires are a special type of fire. They race across open land in hot, dry areas and burn almost everything in their paths. When the weather is hot and dry in a place with lots of fuel, such as dry grasses and bushes, a brush fire will start.

Many people have built homes on dry land that used to be wild. This is because wildland is very beautiful. But there is a high risk of fire in these areas. As more people move into these areas, they risk losing their homes and other buildings to fire. In 2013, a brush fire was ignited by lightning in Arizona. High winds spread the flames until the fire covered 13 square miles (34 km²). More than one hundred homes were destroyed. Nineteen elite firefighters died. They had little time to escape after the wind suddenly changed direction.

Brush fires can move quickly across open, dry land.

4
FIREFIGHTERS AT WORK

Think fast! When firefighters arrive at a forest fire, they must consider where the fire might go and how quickly it will move. We know that fire needs three things to burn: oxygen, fuel, and heat. Firefighters need to remove at least one of these things to put out the fire.

First, the firefighters make a fire line. A fire line is a line made in the ground by clearing away all the fuel, such as leaves and branches. If all the fuel is taken away, the fire cannot spread. A fire line

Firefighters create a fire line to help stop the spread of the fire.

must be wide enough to contain the fire. If it's windy, a fire can jump over the line and spread. Firefighters use tools, such as special axes called **Pulaskis,** to dig fire lines. Next, firefighters spray lots of cold water on the fire to remove the heat.

SMOKE JUMPERS

Sometimes a fire is in a **remote** area. This can make it hard for firefighters to reach the fire by truck, and it may take days to reach it on foot. In 1940, the United States Forest Service started using smoke jumpers. Smoke jumpers are firefighters who **parachute** out of airplanes and land on the ground near the fire. Other parachutes carrying supplies, such as Pulaskis, are sent down with them. If firefighters get to the fire early, they can stop it sooner.

Smoke jumping is very dangerous. Smoke jumpers are specially trained so that they don't get hurt when they are doing their job.

Smoke jumpers bravely parachute into hard-to-reach areas near a burning fire.

5
SUMMER FIRES AT YELLOWSTONE PARK

Yellowstone National Park has a fire season every summer. Many fires start from lightning in the hot, dry weather. The 1988 season was the worst fire season in history. There were 249 fires in the park. About 25,000 firefighters worked all summer, day and night, to stop the fires. Airplanes and helicopters were used to drop water on the fires from above.

The fires were finally put out by an early snowfall. About one million acres (4,047 km²) of

Firefighters in Wyoming take a break from battling the 1988 Yellowstone fires.

Yellowstone had burned. Many people were upset at the loss of parts of this beautiful park. The worst fire that season wasn't caused by lightning. It was caused by people.

LET IT BURN?

In 1972, the National Park Service created a Let It Burn plan for national parks, such as Yellowstone. This means that any fire started by natural causes will be allowed to burn until it goes out on its own. This is because fires are a part of a forest's natural **ecosystem**. When natural fires are stopped by firefighters, changes can occur in the forest that **threaten** the future of the forest. The forest may have trouble protecting itself from future fires. But many people don't like the Let It Burn plan because it takes years for the new trees to grow again after a fire.

This twin-engined water bomber is dropping its load on a forest fire. But in national parks, fires are allowed to burn naturally as part of the natural cycle of the forest.

6

HOW TO PROTECT YOUR HOME

If you live in an area where forest or brush fires happen often, how can you stay safe? There are things you and your family can do to protect your home.

First, be sure to maintain the area around your home in a way that discourages fire. Keep dead branches and leaves away from the house. The **shingles** on your roof should be made of fireproof material.

A 2007 San Diego brush fire destroyed this home. Keep your family safe by following some steps to protect your home from wildfires.

Second, decide with your family on a special meeting place. If there is a fire and you get separated from your family, you'll know to meet at that place.

Last, it's important to never play with matches or fire no matter where you are. Fire is very powerful. Remember what Smokey Bear says: "Only you can prevent forest fires."

Smokey Bear has good advice: only you can prevent a forest fire!

FIRE DANGER

MODERATE

TODAY!

PREVENT WILDFIRES

LEARN MORE

Books

Furgang, Kathy. *Wildfires*. Washington, D.C.: National Geographic Children's Books, 2015.

Mara, Wil. *Smokejumper*. North Mankato, Minn.: Cherry Lake Publishing, 2015.

Merrick, Patrick. *Forest Fires*. North Mankato, Minn.: The Child's World, 2015.

Web Sites

fema.gov/kids

Read more about forest fires.

smokeybear.com/kids

Learn how to prevent forest fires.

INDEX

Published in 2016 by Enslow Publishing, LLC.
101 W. 23rd Street, Suite 240, New York, NY 10011

Library of Congress Cataloging-in-Publication Data
Katirgis, Jane, author.
Fearsome forest fires / Jane Katirgis and Michele Ingber Drohan.
    pages cm. — (Earth's natural disasters)
Summary: "Discusses the science behind forest fires and what to do to stay safe from them"—Provided by publisher.
Audience: Ages 8+
Audience: Grades 4 to 6
Includes bibliographical references and index.
ISBN 978-0-7660-6811-7 (library binding)
ISBN 978-0-7660-6809-4 (pbk.)
ISBN 978-0-7660-6810-0 (6-pack)
1. Forest fires—Juvenile literature. 2. Forest fires—Prevention and control—Juvenile literature. 3. Fire ecology—Juvenile literature. I. Drohan, Michele Ingber, author. II. Title.
SD421.K28 2015
634.9'618—dc23
                        2015008025

Printed in the United States of America

To Our Readers: We have done our best to make sure all Web site addresses in this book were active and appropriate when we went to press. However, the author and the publisher have no control over and assume no liability for the material available on those Web sites or on any Web sites they may link to. Any comments or suggestions can be sent by e-mail to customerservice@enslow.com.

Photo Credits: Arztsamui/Shutterstock.com, p. 4; Bryan Oller/AP Images, p. 7; EpicStockMedia/Shutterstock.com (chapter openers and back matter backgrounds); David White/Photolibrary/Getty Images, p. 8; fStop Images - Julia Christe/Brand X Pictures/Getty Images, p. 17; Images by Ni-ree/Moment/Getty Images, p. 1; Jamie Farrant/Digital Vision Vectors (caption boxes); Kevin Key/Shutterstock.com, p. 27; Lindsay Basson/Shutterstock.com, p. 15; Oleh Slobodeniuk/Moments/Getty Images, p. 11; Photography by Mangiwau/Moment/Getty Images, p. 13; Powell Tribune/AP Images, p. 23; robert cicchetti/Shutterstock.com, p. 29; Sarah Jessup/Shutterstock.com, p. 21; StockPhotosLV/Shutterstock.com, p 19; supergenijalac/Shutterstock.com, p. 25; traffic_analyzer/Digital Vision Vectors/Getty Images (page folios).

Cover Credits: Images by Ni-ree/Moment/Getty Images (fire); EpicStockMedia/Shutterstock.com (background); traffic_analyzer/Digital Vision Vectors/Getty Images (series icon).